The Silent Season: A 1950s Christmas Tale of Love, Loss, and Hope

A Heartwarming Holiday Story of a Widow's Journey Through Grief and the Power of Community in a Small Midwest Town

James Holloway

Epilogue: The Promise of Spring

It wasn't the sound of birdsong that stirred Maggie awake that morning, nor the gentle light filtering through the sheer curtains. It was the unmistakable scent of fresh earth—the rich, loamy promise of spring—that filled her small bedroom. For the first time in what felt like forever, the air had shifted, no longer biting with winter's edge but soft and warm, carrying with it a sense of new beginnings.

She lay still for a moment, letting it wash over her. The long winter had finally ended. The silence that had clung to her life for over a year, since Bill's death, had loosened its grip, replaced by something vibrant, something alive.

Maggie sat up and glanced out the window. The snow had melted, leaving the world damp and glistening. Small patches of green were beginning to break through the frost-bitten ground, and in the distance, the trees that had stood bare and brittle all winter were sprouting their first timid buds. The world outside was waking up—just as she had.

There was a knock at her bedroom door, and before she could answer, Susie burst in, her face flushed with excitement. "Mommy! Mommy! Come see! There's flowers!"

Maggie smiled, her heart swelling at the sight of her daughter's joy. Susie's enthusiasm was infectious, and without a second thought, Maggie slipped out of bed and followed her into the hallway. Tommy was already downstairs, his serious face softened by the warmth of the early morning light that streamed through the kitchen windows.

"They're just crocuses," Tommy said with a shrug, but there was a glimmer of excitement in his eyes. "But it means spring's coming."

Maggie felt her chest tighten with emotion, remembering how long it had been since she had seen that light in Tommy's eyes—the same light that had dimmed after Bill's accident, the same one that had taken so long to return. And now, here it was, as fragile and bright as the first flowers pushing their way through the frost.

Together, they walked out onto the front porch, where the crisp morning air greeted them, still cool but full of possibility. In the yard, small clusters of purple crocuses dotted the patches of grass, their petals open to the weak sunlight. Maggie inhaled deeply, the scent of wet earth and new growth filling her lungs. It felt like renewal—like the world was finally breathing again.

And with it, so was she.

As she stood there, watching her children marvel at the little patches of color springing up around their yard, Maggie heard the familiar sound of footsteps approaching from the lane. She turned, and there was Sam, carrying a bundle of small seedlings in his hands, a grin spreading across his face as he saw her.

"Thought I'd bring these by," he called as he walked up the path, his voice full of the warmth she had come to rely on. "I figured we could start planting today."

Maggie's heart leapt at the sight of him. Sam had become so much more than the quiet friend who had helped her through her darkest days. He had become her partner, in every sense of the word—a steady, comforting presence, a source of strength and hope.

"And here I thought you'd be sleeping in," Maggie teased, her eyes bright with affection.

Sam chuckled, setting the seedlings down on the porch and stepping closer to her. "Not today. It's planting season now. Time to wake up."

Maggie smiled, the words sinking in deeper than he knew. Time to wake up. Time to embrace what was ahead. The winter was over, the season of grief and silence had passed. In its place was something new—something fragile and beautiful, just like the crocuses pushing their way through the soil.

She reached out and took Sam's hand, pulling him gently toward the yard where the children were already exploring. Together, they crouched beside Tommy and Susie, inspecting the small flowers that had appeared as if by magic overnight.

For a long while, they stayed there in the damp earth, planning the garden they would plant together. A garden not just for the spring, but for the summer, the fall—for the years ahead.

And in that moment, Maggie realized that this—this simple, quiet morning in the warmth of spring—was the life she had been waiting for. It wasn't the life she had once imagined with Bill, and it wasn't the life that had been lost to the cold grasp of grief. It was something new, something full of promise, of laughter, of love.

The silent season had given way to a new beginning. And this time, she wasn't afraid.

As the sun climbed higher in the sky, casting the first true warmth of the season over the town, Maggie stood up, her heart full. The promise of spring was all around her, not just in the earth, but in the people she loved—in her children, in Sam, in the quiet strength she had found within herself.

And as she looked out over the yard, she knew with absolute certainty that whatever came next, she would be ready.

Because this time, she wasn't facing it alone.

Chapter 1
The Cold Wind Blows

The wind howled through the narrow streets of the small Midwestern town, carrying with it the first real bite of winter. Margaret "Maggie" Evans pulled her wool coat tighter around her body, her gloved hands gripping the edges of her collar as she hurried home from the corner store. A few brown leaves, the last remnants of autumn, skittered across the frozen pavement, and the air smelled of impending snow. It was early December, but already the cold seemed to settle into her bones, much like the sadness that had become her constant companion.

Maggie had been to town for bread and canned soup—simple things she could stretch into meals for the week. As she walked the familiar path back to the small house she rented on the edge of town, she glanced at the empty storefronts, their windows dark and uninviting. It hadn't always been like this. The streets used to be filled with holiday cheer by now, with shops decked out in garlands and lights, welcoming customers with the promise of Christmas joy. But this year, the windows were bare, the shops mostly closed. The town had lost its heart when the factory shut down earlier that year, and with it, the lifeblood of the community.

James Holloway

She paused in front of what used to be Walker's General Store, now boarded up like so many others. A faded wreath hung lopsided on the door, a relic from last Christmas that had been left behind, forgotten. Maggie stared at it for a moment, her thoughts drifting back to her late husband, Bill. Just last year, he had stood in this very spot, joking with Mr. Walker about the weather while buying a last-minute gift for Tommy—a small train set that still sat in pieces in their living room.

Bill had always loved Christmas. He used to bring the tree home himself, cutting it from the woods just outside of town, and setting it up while Tommy and Susie danced around him in excitement. His laughter had filled their home like warm firelight, chasing away the cold. Now, everything felt different—colder, emptier. It had been a year since the accident at the factory, since Bill had gone to work and never come back.

Maggie shook herself from the memory and turned down Maple Street, the familiar path winding toward home. The wind picked up, and the gray sky above threatened snow, but the world around her seemed as still and silent as a graveyard. A few of the houses were decorated with sparse Christmas lights, but there were no children playing in the yards, no carols drifting through the windows. The town was holding its breath, waiting for a Christmas that might not come.

By the time she reached her front door, Maggie felt the weight of the cold settling into her muscles. She fumbled for her keys, her fingers stiff from the chill, and stepped into the warmth of the small kitchen. The smell of potatoes boiling on the stove greeted her, along with the sound of children's voices from the living room.

"Mommy!" Susie's voice was the first to break through the stillness of the house. The six-year-old appeared in the kitchen doorway, her blonde hair wild around her face and her cheeks flushed from playing. "Tommy's not sharing the crayons!"

The Silent Season: A 1950s Christmas Tale of Love, Loss, and Hope

Maggie managed a tired smile as she set the grocery bag on the counter. "I'm sure you two can work it out, honey."

Tommy, eight years old and too old for such squabbles in his own mind, followed his sister into the kitchen, cradling the crayon box as if it were a prized possession. His serious face softened when he saw his mother's weary expression.

"Sorry, Mom. I'll share," he said, handing the box to Susie, who immediately brightened and scampered back to the living room.

"Thanks, sweetheart," Maggie said, reaching out to ruffle Tommy's hair. He didn't flinch away like he usually did, instead leaning into her touch for a brief moment before turning to follow his sister.

Maggie sighed and moved to the stove, stirring the pot absentmindedly. She glanced at the small table in the corner where Tommy and Susie's drawings of snowmen and reindeer lay scattered, a bright contrast to the muted colors of the kitchen. The air felt thick with quiet, the kind that had settled in since Bill's passing, and no matter how hard she tried to shake it, the silence always returned.

Outside, the wind picked up again, rattling the windows. Maggie could feel it, that same bitter cold creeping into the edges of her mind. She had tried to keep Christmas alive for the children, for Tommy and Susie's sake, but this year, it felt different. The warmth that had once filled their home seemed lost. She couldn't help but feel that without Bill, without his laughter and steady presence, Christmas itself had become a hollow thing.

"Maggie, you've got to pull it together," she muttered under her breath, pushing her hair back from her face as she grabbed bowls from the cupboard. She had been doing her best—working odd jobs where she could find them, stretching their savings to cover rent, food, and whatever small gifts she could afford for the children. But the strain was constant, and the ache of missing Bill gnawed at her

in the quiet moments, when the house was still and the weight of the season pressed down on her.

As she set the table, her mind drifted back to the church and the conversation she'd had with Father O'Leary just that morning. He had mentioned the Christmas pageant, the annual tradition that everyone in town looked forward to. He'd asked if she might be willing to help organize it this year, but she had brushed him off. The idea of Christmas, of celebrating anything, felt so distant from where she was right now. It seemed impossible to embrace the season when her heart was so heavy.

The children's laughter from the other room brought her back to the present. She looked toward the living room, where Tommy and Susie were sitting side by side, drawing with their crayons. They still had their joy, even if she had lost hers. Maybe that was enough for now.

Maggie spooned the thin potato soup into bowls and called the children to the table. As they sat down, Tommy looked up at her, his blue eyes wide with a question that had been building for days.

"Mom," he said, "are we gonna have a Christmas tree this year?"

The words hung in the air between them, and for a moment, Maggie couldn't find her voice. She looked at her son, then at Susie, who was watching her with equal anticipation. How could she explain to them that even the simplest traditions felt overwhelming without Bill?

"I don't know, Tommy," she finally said, her voice quiet. "We'll see."

It was all she could offer.

As they ate in silence, Maggie's mind drifted to the church again, to Father O'Leary's words and the Christmas pageant. The wind outside howled once more, and Maggie wondered if maybe, just maybe, the cold wind could blow something else into her life—

The Silent Season: A 1950s Christmas Tale of Love, Loss, and Hope

something warmer, something brighter. But for now, all she could do was survive the season, one day at a time.

The snow had started falling by the time she tucked the children into bed, covering the town in a soft, white blanket. As she looked out the window, Maggie couldn't help but think that this Christmas would be as silent as the snow itself—quiet, still, and heavy with the weight of everything that had been lost.

And yet, in that silence, there was a flicker of something else, too—something she wasn't quite ready to name. Not yet.

But maybe soon.

Chapter 2
Silent Streets

Maggie woke to the faint sound of wind tapping against the bedroom window, a cold draft slipping through the cracks in the old wooden frame. She pulled the covers tighter around herself, but it did little to stop the chill that had settled in her bones overnight. Outside, the world was covered in a fresh layer of snow, the kind that looked pristine for a few fleeting hours before the day's trudging footsteps and cars turned it into slush. Christmas was less than three weeks away, but there was no sign of it in her heart or in the town.

She lay in bed for a few more minutes, listening to the soft breathing of her children in the next room. The small, shared bedroom where Tommy and Susie slept was just off the kitchen, and if she listened closely, she could hear the familiar sounds of Tommy rolling over in his sleep, Susie's little hums as she dreamed. It was comforting in its own way, and yet it reminded her how fragile their peace really was—how much rested on her shoulders alone now.

The factory had closed in March, the loss of Bill's job devastating, but it had been his death a few months later that had truly broken her. Now, as winter settled into the town like an unwelcome

The Silent Season: A 1950s Christmas Tale of Love, Loss, and Hope

guest, the reality of their situation weighed heavier with each passing day. She had found work where she could—cleaning houses, mending clothes, helping out in the small diner on the weekends—but it was never enough. Christmas was coming, and there was nothing to spare. Not for a tree. Not for presents. Not even for the extra little comforts she'd been able to provide for them last year, before everything had gone wrong.

The house felt colder than usual when she finally forced herself out of bed. In the kitchen, she started a fire in the stove, the warmth slowly creeping through the small house as the smell of burning wood filled the room. She glanced out the window above the sink, watching as the early morning light spread over the snow-covered streets. The town square, once the heart of the community, looked barren and lifeless.

Her thoughts drifted to what it used to be like this time of year. The factory workers would have received their holiday bonuses by now, and the whole town would've been bustling with Christmas preparations. Lights would be strung along the storefronts, the large tree in the center of the square would have been lit, and children would be out playing in the snow, their laughter echoing off the brick buildings. She could still hear Bill's voice in her mind, talking about buying the kids new coats and maybe even a sled. But now, the square stood silent, its shops empty, some closed for good, their windows dark and unwelcoming.

Maggie stirred the embers in the stove and reached for the kettle. As the water heated, her thoughts returned to Father O'Leary's words from the other day.

The Christmas pageant, he had said, his voice gentle yet insistent. *We need someone to help, Maggie. We need you.*

She had brushed him off then, overwhelmed by the very idea of taking on more responsibility. What could she offer the church, or anyone, when she barely had the energy to keep her own family afloat? And yet, she couldn't shake the memory of his kind eyes, the *way he had looked at her as though he understood exactly what she was going through.*

"I don't have time for this," she muttered to herself, pouring the hot water into a chipped teacup. She didn't. Between her odd jobs and keeping the children fed, there wasn't a minute to spare for pageants, or decorations, or anything else that seemed trivial in comparison to just surviving the season.

The sound of footsteps padding into the kitchen interrupted her thoughts. Tommy appeared in the doorway, his hair tousled from sleep, rubbing his eyes. He glanced up at her, blinking against the early morning light.

"Morning, Mom," he mumbled, shuffling over to the stove for warmth.

"Morning, sweetheart," she replied, mustering a smile. "Did you sleep okay?"

"Yeah." He hesitated, then looked at her with a seriousness that felt beyond his eight years. "Mom, do you think there'll be a Christmas pageant this year?"

Maggie paused, her hands frozen in the act of stirring her tea. She had hoped Tommy wouldn't ask, had hoped he wouldn't notice the town's quiet streets and abandoned holiday traditions. But of course, he had. Tommy noticed everything.

"I think so," she said carefully, not wanting to get his hopes up. "Father O'Leary's still planning it, but... things are different this year."

Tommy nodded, though she could see the flicker of disappointment cross his face. He was too young to fully understand the weight of everything that had changed since the factory closed, since his father died. But he felt it. Maggie could see it in the way he had started helping more around the house without being asked, the way he tried to shield Susie from the realities of their situation. He had taken on responsibilities that no child his age should have to carry, and it broke her heart to watch it happen.

The Silent Season: A 1950s Christmas Tale of Love, Loss, and Hope

She ruffled his hair as he sat down at the table. "We'll see, okay? Maybe this year's pageant will be different, but it doesn't mean it won't be special."

Tommy gave a small, understanding nod, and Maggie turned back to her tea, though her mind was far from the warm kitchen. She didn't know how to explain to him that even something as small as a pageant felt impossible right now. The town itself seemed to be giving up, slipping quietly into the cold as if it, too, had lost its will to fight.

Later that morning, Maggie walked to town to check on a potential job—cleaning for an older woman who lived near the edge of the square. As she walked, the streets around her felt unnervingly empty. The few people she did see hurried along, heads down, their faces tight with worry and the bitter cold. No one stopped to chat, no one smiled or waved. The holiday decorations that had once brought the town to life were conspicuously absent, replaced by sagging wreaths and dim, unlit windows.

Maggie passed by the church, its heavy wooden doors shut tight against the wind. She could picture Father O'Leary inside, likely preparing for Sunday service, going through the motions of keeping the community together in the face of mounting hardships. She wondered how he did it—how he found the strength to keep asking people like her to contribute, to help, when it seemed like the town had nothing left to give.

Ahead, in the town square, the large Christmas tree still stood in its place, but it was bare, no lights or ornaments adorning its branches. In previous years, decorating the tree had been a community event, with children hanging handmade ornaments while their parents strung up the lights. But this year, the tree stood cold and silent, a ghost of Christmases past.

Maggie stopped for a moment in front of the tree, feeling the weight of everything pressing down on her. She had lost so much this year—her husband, her sense of stability, her hope for the future

—and now it seemed like the town itself was disappearing, slipping away into the same silence that had filled her home since Bill's passing.

As she stood there, staring at the barren tree, she heard footsteps crunching through the snow behind her.

"Maggie?"

She turned to see Father O'Leary walking toward her, his coat pulled tight against the cold. His face was lined with the same weariness she felt, but there was something else there, too—a quiet determination.

"I was just thinking about you," he said, offering a small smile.

"Were you?" Maggie tried to return the smile but felt it falter.

"I was. I know things have been... difficult." He glanced around the empty square, his eyes lingering on the undecorated tree. "For everyone."

Maggie nodded, unsure of what to say. Father O'Leary had always been a source of comfort for the town, but even he seemed tired now, as if the weight of all their collective grief had finally begun to wear him down.

"I wanted to ask you again," he continued gently. "About the pageant. I know it seems like a small thing, but I think it could mean a lot to the children this year. To the whole town."

Maggie hesitated, feeling the familiar tug of resistance. She didn't have the energy for this—not when she was barely keeping her own family together.

"Father, I—"

"I understand," he interrupted, his voice soft. "I know you've been carrying a lot. But sometimes, when we help others, we help ourselves, too."

The words hung in the cold air between them, and Maggie felt something shift inside her—something small but undeniable. She looked back at the tree, standing bare and cold in the square, and for *the first time, she wondered what it would look like with lights, with ornaments, with a little bit of life brought back to it.*

"I'll think about it," she said finally, her voice quiet.

Father O'Leary smiled, a glimmer of hope in his eyes. "That's all I ask, Maggie. Just think about it."

As she walked away from the square, back toward her small house on the edge of town, Maggie found herself doing just that. Thinking about the pageant. Thinking about the tree. And wondering, for the first time in a long time, if maybe—just maybe—there was still a little bit of Christmas left in this silent season.

Chapter 3
The Christmas Pageant

Maggie stood in the doorway of the church hall, watching the room come to life around her. The smell of wax and pine hung in the air, mingling with the faint scent of mothballs from the old costume trunks that had been dragged out of storage. The children's excited voices bounced off the high ceiling, filling the otherwise drafty space with the kind of chaotic energy only kids could bring.

Susie was among them, sitting on the floor with a small group of other children, already immersed in the task of sorting through old costumes—angel wings bent from years of use, faded shepherd robes, crowns missing a jewel or two. The innocence of it all brought a pang of nostalgia to Maggie's chest, a reminder of her own childhood when she had played an angel in this very pageant years ago. She hadn't thought about it in years, and now, standing here, the memories felt like a lifetime away.

The day after her conversation with Father O'Leary, Helen had shown up at her door with her usual brisk energy, barely giving Maggie a chance to refuse.

The Silent Season: A 1950s Christmas Tale of Love, Loss, and Hope

"You're coming to help," Helen had announced, not leaving room for argument. "The pageant needs you, Maggie, and frankly, you need the pageant."

Helen had been Maggie's best friend for as long as she could remember, and she had always known exactly when to push Maggie in the right direction. Maggie had protested at first, of course—there was too much to do at home, and she couldn't afford to be distracted by something as frivolous as a children's pageant. But Helen hadn't taken no for an answer, and somehow, here she was.

Maggie glanced around the hall, feeling a little out of place among the flurry of activity. The other mothers bustled about, sorting through decorations and making lists of what was still needed for the performance. Despite the patchwork quality of the costumes and the scarcity of decorations, there was a buzz of excitement, a determination to make something beautiful out of what little they had. It was something Maggie couldn't quite feel yet, but she envied it.

Helen appeared by her side, arms full of tinsel that had seen better days. "Look at this place, Maggie," she said, shaking her head with a smile. "It's a disaster, but we'll pull it together somehow."

"I don't even know where to start," Maggie admitted, her voice low as she watched Susie hold up a pair of angel wings, inspecting them like they were the most precious thing in the world.

"You'll figure it out. Start with the small things." Helen dropped the tinsel onto a nearby table and looked at Maggie, her eyes softening. "You're doing this for them, for Susie and Tommy. They need this. And so do you."

Maggie opened her mouth to protest, but Helen cut her off with a wave of her hand.

"I know you're tired, I know things have been hard," Helen said gently, "but I also know you. You don't have to pretend this is easy, but that doesn't mean you can't find some joy in it."

Maggie looked down at the floor, feeling a twinge of guilt for her reluctance. Helen was right—she had spent so much time trying to keep everything together that she had forgotten what it was like to be part of something bigger than her grief. Her children were excited about the pageant. Susie had been talking about it for days now, the enthusiasm in her voice a rare burst of happiness amidst the gloom that had settled over their home.

And Tommy, though quieter about it, had asked her the night before if she thought Dad would have liked to see him play Joseph in the Nativity. The question had pierced her heart, but she had smiled, telling him how proud his father would be. She could see how much Tommy was holding back—trying to be the man of the house in a way no eight-year-old should have to be.

"I just don't know if I have it in me, Helen," Maggie finally admitted, her voice barely above a whisper. "I'm so tired."

Helen's expression softened even more. "I know, honey. But we're all tired. You're not alone in this."

Those words lingered with Maggie as the day went on, especially as she watched the other parents move about the room, their faces etched with the same worry and exhaustion she saw in the mirror every morning. None of them had it easy—the town's economic downturn had hit everyone, and yet here they were, stitching costumes, fixing broken halos, and preparing for the one tradition that seemed to hold the fabric of the town together.

Father O'Leary entered the hall, his arms filled with a box of old decorations, and made his way toward Maggie. "It's looking better already, don't you think?" he asked, his eyes twinkling as he surveyed the room.

Maggie glanced around, noticing how, despite the worn decorations and mismatched costumes, there was a warmth beginning to grow in the room. The children, unaware of the struggles their parents were facing, laughed as they tried on costumes, their excite-

ment infectious. Even the adults seemed to find solace in the shared task, their small conversations punctuated by moments of genuine laughter.

"It's starting to feel like Christmas in here," Maggie admitted, surprising herself with the observation.

Father O'Leary smiled. "That's the spirit I've been hoping to see. It doesn't take much, does it? Just a little effort, a little coming together."

"I suppose not," she said, feeling a flicker of something she hadn't felt in a long time. It wasn't quite joy—not yet—but it was a start.

Susie, still clutching the slightly bent angel wings, ran up to her, eyes wide with excitement. "Mommy! Look at these! Do you think I'll get to wear them?"

Maggie knelt down to her daughter's level, smiling at the eager expression on her face. "We'll see, sweetheart. But you look like a perfect little angel to me."

Susie beamed, her blue eyes sparkling. "I'm gonna practice my lines with Tommy! He says I need to work on my singing too."

Maggie watched as Susie ran back to join the other children, her heart swelling with a mixture of pride and sadness. It felt bittersweet to see Susie so full of life, knowing that Bill should have been here to share in these moments. But even as the ache of his absence settled over her, she felt a small measure of peace watching her children find joy in something as simple as a church pageant.

As the day wore on, Maggie found herself slowly getting drawn into the preparations. She helped Helen patch up an old angel costume, her hands moving in the familiar rhythm of needle and thread, a skill she had learned from her own mother many years ago.

"We're making progress," Helen said, her voice bright as she held up the newly mended costume. "This might just turn out to be a real pageant after all."

Maggie couldn't help but smile. "It's something, that's for sure."

It was then that Sam Walker walked into the hall, carrying a stack of freshly painted wooden props for the Nativity scene. Maggie hadn't seen much of Sam since the factory had closed, though he had been a close friend of Bill's. Seeing him now, with his quiet presence and familiar face, stirred something in her. He looked different—older, wearier—but there was still kindness in his eyes as he set the props down near the stage.

He caught her gaze and smiled softly. "I hear you're helping with the pageant this year."

"I was... persuaded," Maggie said, nodding toward Helen, who waved from across the room.

Sam chuckled. "That sounds about right. Well, it's good to see you, Maggie. It's been a while."

"It has." She hesitated, unsure of what else to say. There was an unspoken understanding between them—both had lost something when the factory shut down, both were trying to find their way forward in the same bleak winter.

Before either could say more, Father O'Leary called for everyone's attention. "I think that's enough for today," he said, his voice ringing through the hall. "Thank you all for your hard work. We'll meet again next week for the final preparations."

As the parents and children began to gather their things, Maggie watched Sam from across the room as he quietly helped one of the younger boys untangle a string of lights. There was something steady about him, something that gave her a sense of calm. For the first time in months, Maggie felt like she wasn't the only one carrying the weight of loss.

Later that evening, as she tucked Susie into bed, Maggie found herself thinking about the pageant again. There was still so much to do, and yet, somehow, it didn't seem as overwhelming as it had

The Silent Season: A 1950s Christmas Tale of Love, Loss, and Hope

before. Maybe Helen was right—maybe being part of this, of something bigger than her own grief, was what she needed after all.

As she stood in the doorway of her children's bedroom, watching them drift off to sleep, Maggie felt the flicker of hope return, faint but undeniable.

Christmas was coming. And this year, it might just bring a little light with it.

Chapter 4
The Weight of Loss

The sound of children's laughter echoed faintly in Maggie's mind as she walked back home from the church that evening. The cold December air had a way of waking her up, sharp and unforgiving, but today, it felt different—heavier. The warmth of the church hall and the pageant preparations lingered with her, but so did the shadow of Bill's absence. For the first time in a long while, she had allowed herself to feel a spark of hope, to let in a little joy. But now, as the dark streets swallowed her in their winter stillness, the old weight settled back on her shoulders like a familiar burden.

The walk from the church to her small home wasn't far, but tonight, each step felt longer, as if she were wading through a memory. The houses she passed were dimly lit, the occasional flicker of a Christmas candle visible through the frosted windows. But there were no grand displays, no colorful lights strung across porches, no wreaths on the doors. The town, once brimming with life and holiday cheer, had fallen into silence just like she had.

Maggie pulled her coat tighter against the chill and crossed the street, her thoughts wandering back to the pageant. Susie had been

The Silent Season: A 1950s Christmas Tale of Love, Loss, and Hope

so excited today, her face glowing with happiness as she practiced her lines with Tommy. It was a rare thing, seeing both of her children like that—joyful, alive, unburdened by the weight of the world that had pressed down on them since Bill's accident.

The house came into view, its silhouette dark against the snowy street, and Maggie's heart sank a little. The Christmas lights Bill had strung up each year lay in a tangled heap in the attic, untouched. There was no tree, no decoration to mark the season. It wasn't just that she couldn't afford them this year—it was the emotional effort. She couldn't bring herself to face the rituals of Christmas without him.

Bill's absence was a hollow ache that no amount of tinsel or ornaments could fill. The memory of his hands carefully hanging ornaments with the children, laughing as Susie tried to balance a star too big for the little tree they could afford, haunted her. Those memories, once so sweet, now felt like a heavy weight dragging her down.

As she opened the front door, the warmth of the small house did little to chase away the chill inside her. Tommy and Susie were still awake, sitting by the fireplace with their crayons and paper, drawing pictures of angels and shepherds for the pageant.

"Mommy, look!" Susie called, holding up a crayon drawing of herself as an angel, complete with glittery wings and a halo. "Do you think I'll get to wear the gold wings?"

Maggie forced a smile, kneeling next to her daughter. "It's beautiful, sweetheart. I'm sure you'll look just like that in the pageant."

Susie beamed, satisfied, and returned to her drawing, while Tommy quietly added finishing touches to his own picture of the Nativity scene. Maggie watched them for a moment, her heart swelling with pride and love. They were doing their best to carry on, to find happiness in the small things, despite everything that had changed. And yet, she couldn't shake the feeling that she was failing them—failing to give them the Christmas they deserved, the Christmas Bill would have wanted for them.

After tucking them into bed, Maggie made herself a cup of tea and sat by the window, staring out into the quiet night. Snow had begun to fall again, soft and silent, covering the streets in a delicate blanket of white. It was beautiful, in a way, but also too quiet—too still. She found herself thinking about the factory, about how different things had been before it closed down.

Bill had worked there for nearly a decade, along with most of the other men in town. It had been more than a job—it was the town's heartbeat. Without it, everything had started to wither. And when the accident happened—when Bill was taken from her—it felt like the final blow. The factory had closed its doors for good not long after, leaving everyone scrambling to find work, to make ends meet. The closure hadn't just taken their jobs, it had taken their sense of security, their sense of identity.

Maggie closed her eyes, trying to block out the flood of memories that came rushing back. She could still see Bill's face that morning, the way he had kissed her on the cheek before leaving for work. She could still hear the phone call, still remember the way her knees had buckled when she heard the words. The accident had been sudden, senseless. A piece of faulty equipment. That was all it took to shatter her world.

She wiped at her eyes, angry at herself for crying again. It had been a year—long enough, surely, to start moving forward. But the grief clung to her like a second skin, always just beneath the surface, threatening to pull her under when she least expected it. She had thought she could manage it by keeping herself busy, by focusing on the children, by shutting out the reminders of Christmas. But now, with the pageant looming, with the town slowly coming back to life around her, she felt like she was being pulled in two directions— toward the light of the season and the darkness of her grief.

Her thoughts drifted to Sam Walker, who had been at the

The Silent Season: A 1950s Christmas Tale of Love, Loss, and Hope

church today, quietly working on the Nativity scene props. He had lost his job at the factory, too, and she knew he was struggling just as much as she was. And yet, there was something steady about him—something that gave her comfort. He had lost, too. He understood. And somehow, seeing him working, smiling at the children, had made her feel a little less alone.

Maggie sighed and looked at the empty space in the corner of the living room where the Christmas tree used to go. She could almost see it—Bill, untangling the lights, Tommy and Susie dancing around him in excitement, the room filled with the smell of pine and laughter.

But now the corner was bare. And so was she.

As the tea cooled in her hands, Maggie found herself wondering if maybe she was wrong—maybe the pageant was exactly what she needed, not just for the children, but for herself. Maybe there was something to Father O'Leary's words about finding solace in community, in doing something beyond herself, even if it was just helping put together a children's Christmas play.

The grief wasn't going to go away—she knew that now. It was part of her, woven into every moment of her life. But maybe, just maybe, she could carry it differently. Maybe she could let a little bit of Christmas in, not for Bill's sake, but for her own.

The sound of the children's soft breathing filled the house as Maggie stood up from the window and padded toward the small closet where they kept the Christmas decorations. She opened the door slowly, her heart pounding as she reached for the old box of ornaments that had sat untouched since last year.

Inside, she found the familiar glass baubles, the homemade paper stars, and at the very top, the angel that always went on the tree. Bill had insisted on putting it up himself every year, lifting Susie up to help place it just right. The memory stung, but as Maggie held the delicate angel in her hands, she felt a flicker of something else—a quiet resolve.

Maybe this year, the tree wouldn't be as grand, the presents wouldn't be as many, and the laughter wouldn't be as full. But there would still be Christmas. For the children. For herself. And maybe, for Bill, too.

The next day, Maggie made her way to town again. She had decided it was time. Time to get involved, time to let the pageant be more than just another task. It was time to let some of the spirit back in, even if it hurt. Even if it wasn't the same.

As she walked through the snow-covered streets, past the silent storefronts and barren windows, Maggie caught sight of Father O'Leary outside the church, hanging a simple wreath on the door. He looked up and smiled when he saw her approaching, his breath visible in the cold air.

"Maggie," he said, his voice warm and familiar. "I was just thinking about you."

She smiled faintly, the wind brushing her cheeks with a biting chill. "I've decided to help with the pageant," she said, her voice steady despite the knot of emotion in her throat. "I can't promise I'll be much use, but... I'll be there."

Father O'Leary's face brightened with a gentle, understanding smile. "That's all we need. A little bit of hope goes a long way."

Maggie nodded, her heart heavy but lighter than it had been in months. As she turned toward the church, toward the preparations that lay ahead, she felt something new—a small, fragile flicker of light in the dark.

And for the first time since Bill's death, Maggie allowed herself to believe that maybe, just maybe, there could be a way forward. Even if it was slow, even if it was quiet, there could still be hope.

And there could still be Christmas.

Chapter 5
A Helping Hand

The winter sun barely broke through the overcast sky as Maggie made her way toward the church. The snow from the previous night had settled in soft, uneven patches on the streets, and her boots crunched against the thin layer of ice beneath. The town felt as muted as ever, but something inside her had shifted since she'd made the decision to help with the Christmas pageant. There was a faint sense of purpose now, a reason to get up and out of the house beyond the daily tasks of survival.

As she approached the church, the sound of hammering greeted her—steady, rhythmic thuds that echoed through the crisp air. She followed the sound around the side of the building and found Sam Walker, hunched over a workbench, repairing a broken star that would top the town's modest Christmas tree.

He didn't notice her at first, his attention focused on the wood and nails in front of him. His brow furrowed in concentration, and Maggie hesitated, unsure if she should interrupt. There was something peaceful about the way he worked—methodical, careful, as if this small task was of the utmost importance. She watched for a moment, appreciating the calm that radiated from him, a stark contrast to the turmoil that often filled her own mind.

"Sam," she finally called, stepping forward.

He looked up, startled but quickly smiling when he saw her. "Maggie. I didn't hear you come up."

"I didn't want to interrupt," she said, returning his smile. "You seemed busy."

Sam wiped his hands on his worn work pants and stood up straight, brushing a bit of sawdust from his coat. "Just trying to fix this old thing. It's seen better days." He gestured to the wooden star, the edges splintered and one point completely missing.

"It looks like it's coming together," Maggie offered, stepping closer to get a better look. The star was far from perfect, but the care Sam was putting into it was evident. "You've always been good with your hands."

He shrugged modestly. "It's nothing fancy. Just a little patchwork." His voice softened, and for a moment, they stood in companionable silence, the cold air settling between them.

Maggie shifted on her feet, feeling the weight of unspoken words between them. She hadn't really talked to Sam much since Bill's death. They had exchanged pleasantries at church or around town, but that was all. Bill and Sam had been close, working together at the factory for years, but since the accident, Sam had kept his distance. She didn't blame him—grief had a way of making things awkward, of building invisible walls between people who once shared a common world. Still, standing here with him now, she felt that same quiet understanding she'd noticed before. Sam was grieving too, not just for Bill but for the life they had all lost when the factory closed.

"How are you holding up?" Sam asked, his voice low but gentle.

Maggie hesitated, unsure of how to answer. The truth was, she wasn't sure how she was holding up. Some days felt manageable, like she could push through the fog of grief and make it to the next one. Other days, the weight of Bill's absence pressed down on her so hard it was difficult to breathe. But how could she explain that to someone who was struggling just as much?

"I'm managing," she said finally, her voice quieter than she intended. "Some days are harder than others."

Sam nodded, his eyes reflecting a shared understanding. "Yeah, I get that."

Another silence settled over them, this one more comfortable, as if neither of them needed to fill it with words. The sounds of the world around them—children playing in the distance, the wind rustling through the bare trees—filled the space instead.

"I've been thinking about Bill a lot lately," Sam said suddenly, his voice thick with emotion. "He was a good man. One of the best."

Maggie swallowed hard, her throat tightening at the mention of her husband's name. It was still so strange, hearing other people talk about him in the past tense, as if he were a chapter that had already closed. But hearing Sam say it, there was something comforting in the way he spoke about Bill, something real. He wasn't tiptoeing around her grief, pretending it didn't exist, the way so many others did.

"He was," Maggie agreed softly, her gaze dropping to the ground. "It's been hard without him."

Sam nodded again, his expression somber. "I think about him all the time. Especially when I'm working on something. We used to talk about building things together once we retired. You know, open a little workshop or something."

Maggie's breath caught. Bill had spoken about those dreams often, too—how one day, when the kids were older, he and Sam would start their own little business. She hadn't thought about those conversations in months, not since the accident had stolen that future from them.

"Yeah," she said, her voice barely above a whisper. "He used to talk about that."

For a moment, they both stood there, the weight of all they had lost hanging in the air between them. But then, as if sensing that they were nearing a place too painful to linger, Sam cleared his throat and gestured to the star he had been working on.

"I'm hoping this thing will hold up for the tree this year," he said, his voice lighter now. "The church's decorations are looking pretty sad, but Father O'Leary's determined to make this Christmas special somehow."

Maggie smiled faintly. "He does have a way of bringing people together."

"That he does," Sam agreed, picking up his hammer again. "I suppose we all need something to hold on to."

Maggie nodded, her gaze drifting toward the small churchyard where the tree would be displayed. It wasn't much—just a modest pine, nothing compared to the grand displays she had seen in bigger towns—but it was theirs. It was a symbol of something more than their struggles, more than the loss they all carried.

"Do you need any help with that?" *Maggie asked, surprising herself with the offer. She had come here with the intention of working inside the church, helping with costumes or props, but suddenly, the idea of working with her hands felt like the right thing to do.*

Sam raised an eyebrow. "You want to help with the star?"

"Why not?" Maggie shrugged. "I could use something to keep my mind busy."

Sam smiled, handing her a piece of sandpaper. "I'm not going to turn down the help."

For the next hour, they worked side by side, sanding down the rough edges of the star, patching up the splintered wood, and talking about little things—the weather, the children, the pageant. It wasn't the kind of conversation that carried deep meaning, but it felt good. It felt normal. And for the first time in a long time, Maggie didn't feel like she was drowning in her grief.

The Silent Season: A 1950s Christmas Tale of Love, Loss, and Hope

As they worked, Maggie found herself watching Sam out of the corner of her eye. He moved with the same quiet determination that Bill had always admired in him. There was a steadiness to him, a strength that wasn't loud or boastful, but comforting. He had been through his own share of losses—losing his job, his plans for the future—but he wasn't bitter. If anything, he seemed more focused on helping others, on giving back to the community in the small ways he could.

When they finished sanding the star, Sam stepped back and wiped his hands on his pants, surveying their work.

"I think it'll do," he said with a nod of satisfaction.

Maggie smiled. "It looks good."

Sam glanced at her, his eyes warm. "Thanks for helping, Maggie. It's... it's nice to not do everything alone."

Maggie felt a pang of recognition at his words. She had been doing everything alone for so long—raising the kids, keeping the house together, grieving. She hadn't realized how much she needed someone else, even for something as small as this.

"It is," she agreed softly. "We're not meant to do it all alone, are we?"

"No," Sam said, his voice quiet. "We're not."

They stood there for a moment, the silence between them no longer heavy, but something else—something lighter, more hopeful. Maggie felt it for the first time in months—a sense of connection, of belonging. Sam wasn't Bill, and he never could be. But he was here, and maybe, in some small way, that was enough.

As they packed up the tools and prepared to head inside the church for the rest of the pageant preparations, Maggie felt a flicker of something she hadn't felt in a long time: gratitude. Not just for Sam's help, but for the way the community was slowly, quietly coming together. The way people were showing up for each other, even in the face of so much loss.

She glanced at Sam as they walked back toward the church, the repaired star cradled carefully in his hands. He met her gaze and gave her a small smile, one that seemed to say, We're going to be okay.

And for the first time in a long time, Maggie believed it might be true.

Chapter 6
The Spirit of the Season

The church was a flurry of activity when Maggie and Sam stepped inside, the warmth from the stove in the corner mingling with the smell of pine and the faint scent of beeswax candles. The tables were cluttered with homemade decorations—crocheted angels, paper snowflakes, and mismatched ornaments that had been used and reused over the years. Maggie could hear the children practicing their lines for the Nativity play in the next room, their excited voices rising and falling in the familiar rhythm of rehearsals.

It was an unusual sight. Despite the town's recent struggles, the room hummed with a quiet resilience, as if the people inside had made an unspoken agreement to create something beautiful out of their shared hardship. Maggie had always thought Christmas was about the big gestures—the lights, the presents, the perfectly decorated tree. But here, surrounded by faded decorations and patched-together costumes, she was starting to realize that the spirit of the season came from something much deeper.

Sam set the repaired star on the table, and Father O'Leary appeared almost instantly, his eyes lighting up when he saw it. "You *fixed it!"* he exclaimed, clapping Sam on the shoulder. *"I knew you could."*

Sam shrugged modestly, glancing at Maggie. *"It wasn't just me. Maggie helped."*

Father O'Leary turned to her with a warm smile. *"Thank you, Maggie. I can't tell you how much this means to the community."*

Maggie felt her cheeks flush slightly under his kind gaze. *"It was nothing,"* she said, though the truth was, it hadn't felt like nothing. Working with Sam, being part of the pageant preparations, had been a small step out of the darkness she'd been living in since Bill's death.

The priest turned his attention to the room around them, his face glowing with quiet pride. *"Look at this place,"* he said, almost to himself. *"It may not be the grandest Christmas, but it's ours."*

Maggie followed his gaze, taking in the sight of the townspeople gathered together—some chatting quietly as they stitched costumes, others hanging garlands made of old ribbons and cranberries, children laughing as they tried on their angel wings and shepherd robes. It wasn't perfect, not by a long shot, but there was a warmth here that hadn't existed in town for months. People were pulling together, sharing what little they had to make the holiday special.

Maggie found herself watching Helen, who was busy organizing the makeshift Nativity costumes, her hands moving quickly as she mended a tear in one of the shepherd's cloaks. Helen had always been the practical one, the force that kept things moving. It was Helen who had insisted Maggie get involved, who had reminded her that Christmas wasn't just about surviving—it was about coming together, even when everything else felt like it was falling apart.

"You see it, don't you?" Helen's voice cut through Maggie's thoughts as she glanced up from her sewing. *"The way people are coming together?"*

The Silent Season: A 1950s Christmas Tale of Love, Loss, and Hope

Maggie nodded, her eyes softening. "I do. I didn't think... I didn't think it would feel like this."

Helen raised an eyebrow, giving her a knowing look. "What did you expect?"

"I don't know," Maggie admitted. "I guess I thought it would be harder. More painful."

Helen nodded, her expression understanding. "Grief doesn't go away, Maggie. But it doesn't mean you can't find joy in other things. In this."

Maggie looked around the room again, taking in the scene—the neighbors who had come together to share what little they had, the children's laughter, the warmth that seemed to spread like a quiet, unseen fire. She realized Helen was right. It wasn't about pushing away the pain or pretending it wasn't there. It was about making space for something else. Something better.

The sound of the children singing in the next room drifted through the open door, their sweet, off-key voices filling the church with the familiar strains of Silent Night. Maggie's heart ached at the sound, the bittersweet mix of loss and hope settling in her chest. She could picture Bill in this moment, standing beside her with his arm around her waist, listening to the children with a soft smile on his face. He had always loved Christmas—loved the traditions, the decorations, the pageantry of it all.

Maggie blinked back the tears that threatened to rise, forcing herself to stay present. Bill was gone, but the love he had for this season didn't have to be. She could carry it forward, even if it looked different now. Even if it hurt.

"Maggie?"

She looked up to see Sam standing in front of her, holding a small box of decorations. "I was just thinking," he said, his voice tentative. "We could use some help hanging these up around the church. If you're not too busy?"

Maggie smiled, grateful for the distraction. "Of course. I'd be happy to help."

The two of them worked side by side, stringing up the simple decorations around the edges of the room—garlands made from scraps of fabric, paper ornaments that had clearly been made by the children, and the old wooden star that Sam had repaired. As they worked, they talked in quiet tones, their conversation meandering between small things—how Susie was excited to play an angel, how Tommy was nervous about remembering his lines as Joseph.

And then, without warning, Sam said, "I miss him, you know. Bill."

Maggie froze, her hands stilling on the garland she was pinning to the wall. She hadn't expected Sam to mention Bill, hadn't expected the raw honesty in his voice. She turned to face him, her heart tightening.

"I miss him too," she said softly. "Every day."

Sam nodded, his gaze drifting to the floor. "It's strange, isn't it? How someone can be such a big part of your life and then, all of a sudden... they're just gone."

Maggie swallowed hard, the familiar lump of grief rising in her throat. "Yeah. It's strange."

For a moment, they stood in silence, the air between them thick with the shared weight of loss. But then Sam looked up, meeting her eyes with a soft, sad smile. "But you're doing it, Maggie. You're getting through it. And that's... that's something."

Maggie felt a warmth spread through her chest, something like gratitude. Sam didn't have to say it, but she knew he understood. They were both carrying the same weight, both trying to find a way forward without knowing exactly how. And somehow, being here, together, in this small church with its patchwork decorations and crooked star, made the burden feel a little lighter.

As the afternoon wore on, the preparations for the pageant continued. Maggie found herself getting more and more involved—

helping the children with their lines, hanging up the last of the decorations, listening to Father O'Leary as he made plans for the modest post-pageant gathering. There would be no grand feast this year, no fancy gifts or extravagant celebrations, but there would be warmth. There would be togetherness. And for Maggie, that was starting to feel like enough.

Later, as the sun began to set and the last of the children were bundled up to go home, Father O'Leary called the small group of volunteers together. His face was bright, despite the exhaustion that lingered in his eyes. "Thank you all for your hard work," he said, his voice filled with quiet pride. "I know this has been a difficult year for many of us, but you've shown that even in hard times, we can still come together. We can still find joy."

Maggie stood among the small crowd, her heart swelling with a quiet sense of accomplishment. It wasn't just about the pageant anymore. It was about the town. The people. The way they had come together to create something, even in the face of hardship.

As she left the church that evening, the cold night air biting at her cheeks, Maggie found herself thinking about the days ahead. Christmas Eve was just around the corner, and with it, the pageant that had brought her and so many others back to life, in small but meaningful ways. For the first time in months, she felt something she hadn't allowed herself to feel since Bill died: hope.

And it wasn't the big, overwhelming kind of hope she had always imagined. It was something smaller, quieter. But it was there, flickering at the edges of her grief, making space for light in the darkness.

And as Maggie walked home through the silent streets, her breath visible in the cold air, she found herself smiling—a real smile, one she hadn't felt in a long, long time.

Christmas was coming, and maybe, just maybe, it was bringing a little bit of healing with it.

James Holloway

40

Chapter 7
A Quiet Christmas

*C**hristmas Eve arrived with a soft snowfall, blanketing the small town in a delicate layer of white. The kind of snow that muffled every sound, making the world feel more peaceful, more sacred. Maggie stood in her kitchen, looking out the window as the flakes drifted lazily to the ground. Inside, the house was warm, and the faint smell of baking cookies filled the air. It was a quiet morning, but there was a sense of anticipation that hadn't been there in years.*

The church's Christmas pageant was only hours away, and for the first time since Bill's death, Maggie felt something close to excitement. The preparations over the last few weeks had stirred something in her, something that went beyond the pageant itself. It wasn't just about the decorations or the rehearsals—it was about feeling connected again. To her children, to her neighbors, to herself.

"Mommy, can I wear my angel wings to the pageant?" Susie's voice piped up from the living room, where she was carefully practicing her lines.

Maggie smiled and turned away from the window. "Not until

we get to the church, sweetheart. You don't want to wrinkle them, do you?"

Susie shook her head, her blonde curls bouncing. "No! I want them to be perfect!"

"They will be," Maggie assured her, walking over to kneel next to her daughter. Susie's small face was lit with joy, the excitement for the pageant all she could talk about for days now.

Tommy, who had been sitting at the kitchen table quietly reading, looked up. He had been more reserved about the whole thing, nervous about playing Joseph, but Maggie could tell he was proud. He had memorized every line, practiced every moment, and though he tried to hide it, she could see the flicker of happiness in his eyes.

"You're going to do great, Tommy," Maggie said, reaching over to ruffle his hair.

He gave her a shy smile, ducking his head. "Thanks, Mom. I hope so."

"You've worked hard. I know you will."

For a moment, everything felt almost normal, as if the shadow of loss that had hovered over them for so long had lifted, if only slightly. Christmas was still hard without Bill, but today, it felt less like an absence and more like a memory she could hold in her heart, gently, without the sharp edges.

By the time they made their way to the church later that afternoon, the snowfall had lightened, leaving a pristine layer of white on the ground. Maggie walked hand in hand with Susie and Tommy, their small, bundled-up forms beside her as they headed toward the brightly lit church.

The building was glowing, the modest decorations they had all worked so hard on casting a warm, golden light into the early evening. The little pine tree they had adorned stood proudly outside, its branches dusted with snow and its lights twinkling softly against the gathering dusk. The star Sam had fixed shone brightly at the top, a symbol of something resilient and strong.

The Silent Season: A 1950s Christmas Tale of Love, Loss, and Hope

Maggie's breath caught in her throat as they entered the church. The space, once cold and bare, had been transformed. The homemade garlands, the repaired props, the simple decorations—all of it had come together in a way that felt magical, not because it was perfect, but because it was enough. There was something about the imperfections—the patched costumes, the slightly crooked manger, the children's mismatched halos—that made it all the more beautiful.

The church was filling up, the townspeople arriving with their families, bundled against the cold, their faces bright with the quiet joy of the season. There was no fanfare, no grand celebration. But there was warmth. There was community.

Maggie helped Susie into her angel costume, smoothing out the wings and adjusting the glittery halo as Susie wiggled with excitement.

"Do I look like a real angel?" Susie asked, her wide blue eyes shining.

"The most beautiful angel I've ever seen," Maggie said, her heart swelling.

As the pageant began, Maggie found her seat in the pews near the front, watching with quiet pride as the children filed onto the makeshift stage. Susie was radiant in her angel costume, her small voice ringing out confidently as she recited her lines. Tommy, though serious and composed as Joseph, played his part with care, his voice steady and clear.

The Nativity scene unfolded in front of her, simple yet full of meaning. As the children acted out the story of the first Christmas, Maggie felt a wave of emotion wash over her. The carols, the familiar words, the sight of her children so fully immersed in the spirit of the season—it all tugged at her heart in a way that she hadn't allowed herself to feel in a long time.

But with that emotion came the grief, too. Bill wasn't here to see this. He wasn't sitting beside her, watching their children, his arm around her, his laughter echoing in the church. The absence of him, so sharply felt all year, was ever-present. She missed him deeply, in a way that words could never fully capture.

Halfway through the performance, Maggie quietly slipped out of the pew and stepped outside. The cold air hit her immediately, sharp and biting against her cheeks, but it also cleared her mind. She wrapped her coat tighter around herself and made her way to the side of the church, where the dim lights from the windows cast long shadows on the snow.

She found a bench beneath a tree, the bare branches reaching toward the sky, and sat down, letting the quiet of the night settle around her. The muffled sounds of the children singing drifted out from the church behind her, but for a moment, she just sat in the stillness, letting the tears she had held back finally fall.

It wasn't the overwhelming grief she had felt in the months after Bill's death. It was softer now, quieter. The ache was still there, but it wasn't crushing her. It was part of her, woven into the fabric of who she was, but tonight, in this moment, it felt like something she could carry.

"Maggie?"

She looked up, startled, to see Sam standing a few feet away, his breath visible in the cold air. He looked hesitant, as if he wasn't sure if he should interrupt, but there was a kindness in his eyes that made Maggie's heart ease a little.

"Mind if I join you?" he asked.

Maggie shook her head, and Sam sat down beside her on the bench. They sat in silence for a moment, watching the snow fall softly around them, the quiet enveloping them like a blanket.

"Pageant's going well," Sam said after a while, his voice low and calm.

Maggie nodded. "The kids are doing a great job."

Sam smiled, his gaze drifting toward the church. "Your kids... they're really something, Maggie. You should be proud."

The Silent Season: A 1950s Christmas Tale of Love, Loss, and Hope

"I am," she said softly. "I just... I wish Bill could see them. He would have loved this."

"I know he would've," Sam said quietly. "But he's still here, Maggie. In them. In you. In all of this."

Maggie didn't say anything for a moment, her heart full. She knew Sam understood. He had lost too—his job, his own future plans—and yet here he was, carrying on, helping where he could, showing up for the community. For her.

"I didn't think I could do Christmas this year," Maggie admitted, her voice barely above a whisper. "I didn't think I could feel... anything."

"But you are," Sam said, his voice gentle. "You're here. You're doing it."

Maggie let out a long breath, watching it disappear into the cold night. "I guess I am."

They sat in silence for a while longer, the snow falling softly around them, the quiet punctuated only by the distant sound of carols coming from the church. Maggie felt a warmth beside her—Sam's presence steady and solid, a reminder that she wasn't alone. Not in her grief, not in her healing.

After a few minutes, Sam reached into his coat pocket and pulled out a small, wrapped bundle, holding it out to her. "I wanted to give you this. It's... not much, but I thought you might like it."

Maggie looked at him in surprise, her heart fluttering as she took the gift from his hands. She unwrapped it carefully, revealing a small, handmade ornament—a simple wooden heart, carved with care and polished until it gleamed. The edges were rough, imperfect, but it was beautiful in its simplicity.

"Sam, I..." Maggie's voice trailed off, emotion choking her words. She looked up at him, her eyes shining with gratitude. "Thank you."

"It's just a small thing," Sam said quietly, his eyes warm. "But I *wanted you to have it. Something to remind you that... there's still hope. Even in all of this."*

Maggie stared at the ornament for a moment, turning it over in her hands, feeling the weight of it. It was a symbol, she realized—a symbol of survival, of the quiet strength it took to carry on. It wasn't about replacing what she had lost, but about finding a way forward, even with the scars.

"Thank you, Sam," she said again, her voice steadier this time. "It means more than you know."

Sam smiled softly, his eyes filled with understanding. "You're not alone, Maggie. Not anymore."

As they sat there together in the quiet night, Maggie felt something shift inside her. The grief was still there, but alongside it, there was something else—a sense of healing, of hope. It wasn't the kind of hope that erased the pain, but the kind that made it possible to keep going.

The sound of the final carol drifted out from the church, the children's voices soft and sweet as they sang O Holy Night. Maggie stood, her heart full as she looked down at the small ornament in her hand.

Maybe Christmas didn't have to be perfect. Maybe it didn't have to be the same as it had been before. Maybe it could be something quieter, something different. And maybe that was enough.

As she and Sam made their way back inside, Maggie felt the warmth of the church envelop her once more, the sounds of the children and the townspeople filling the air with a quiet joy. It wasn't a grand celebration, but it was full of love, of togetherness, of hope.

And for the first time in a long time, Maggie felt ready to be part of it. Ready to carry on. Ready to let the spirit of Christmas in.

Even in the silence, there was light.

And maybe, just maybe, that was the greatest gift of all.

Chapter 8
The Gift of Grace

The night was clear and cold as Maggie stood outside the church, watching her breath rise in soft clouds in the still air. The pageant was over, the children had performed beautifully, and the church was now filled with townspeople lingering, sharing quiet conversations and warm cups of cider. The glow of candles flickered through the frosted windows, and from inside, she could hear the faint sound of someone softly playing the piano. It was a peaceful moment, a pause in time that felt precious and rare.

But Maggie needed the quiet, needed a moment to herself to process everything that had unfolded in the last few hours. She stepped away from the warmth and cheer inside, finding solace under the blanket of stars that stretched across the sky above her. The snow crunched beneath her boots as she made her way to the bench under the old oak tree, the same spot where she had sat the night of the pageant rehearsal, when the weight of grief had nearly overwhelmed her.

Tonight, though, the weight felt different. It was still there, but lighter, like she could finally breathe under it. She had watched

Susie glow with happiness in her angel costume, had seen Tommy proudly deliver his lines as Joseph, and for the first time since Bill's death, Maggie had felt... proud. Not just of her children, but of herself. She had made it through. She had done this, despite the sorrow, despite the exhaustion. She had given her children a Christmas, not the one she had always envisioned, but one filled with love and warmth—and that was enough.

She sat on the bench, her hands tucked into her coat pockets, and tilted her head back to look up at the stars. They seemed brighter tonight, like the world itself was giving her a sign that everything would be okay. She had survived the worst year of her life, and now, for the first time, she believed that there might be something more ahead. Something better.

The soft sound of footsteps approaching pulled her out of her thoughts. She turned to see Sam making his way toward her, his coat pulled tightly around him to block out the cold. He didn't say anything as he approached, just gave her that quiet, understanding smile she had come to recognize. Without asking, he sat down beside her on the bench, close enough for his warmth to reach her but leaving enough space between them to make the moment feel comfortable, not pressing.

For a while, they just sat there in silence, watching the stars and the soft glow of the church lights behind them. The town was quiet, the streets nearly deserted, and the only sound was the faint whisper of the wind through the trees. It felt like the world had paused, giving them this moment to simply be.

"Did you see the way Susie lit up on that stage?" Sam asked finally, breaking the silence, his voice soft and full of warmth.

Maggie smiled, her heart swelling with pride again at the thought of her daughter. "She was so excited. I thought she was going to fly away with those wings."

"And Tommy," Sam added, "he did a great job. You should be proud of them. Both of them."

The Silent Season: A 1950s Christmas Tale of Love, Loss, and Hope

"I am," Maggie said, her voice catching slightly. "More than I can even say."

They lapsed into silence again, the weight of their shared grief hanging between them, though tonight it didn't feel so heavy. It felt bearable, like they had finally reached a place where they could carry it together, instead of each shouldering it alone. Maggie had always thought she needed to be strong for her children, for herself. But sitting here with Sam, she realized that strength wasn't something she had to carry by herself.

"I didn't think I could get through Christmas this year," Maggie admitted quietly, her eyes still fixed on the stars. "I thought it would hurt too much."

"I know," Sam said softly. "I felt the same way."

Maggie glanced at him, her heart aching at the thought of the quiet pain he had carried, too. They hadn't talked much about his own losses, about what it had been like for him after the factory closed, after Bill's death. But she knew. She could see it in the way he moved, in the quiet determination with which he worked, in the way he helped others while keeping his own pain tucked away.

"I never thanked you," Maggie said, her voice low but steady. "For being here. For helping. I don't think I would've made it without you."

Sam looked at her, his eyes warm and full of understanding. "You didn't need me, Maggie. You were stronger than you realized. You always were."

Maggie felt her throat tighten, but this time, the tears that came weren't from sadness. They were from gratitude. From the quiet relief of knowing that she wasn't alone. That she didn't have to do this alone.

She reached into her coat pocket and pulled out the small wooden heart that Sam had given her the night of the pageant rehearsal. She held it in her palm, feeling the smooth surface of the wood, the weight of it light but comforting.

"I think this is the most meaningful gift I've ever gotten," she said softly, turning the heart over in her hand. "It's not just about Bill or the past. It's about the future, too."

Sam nodded, his gaze fixed on the small ornament in her hand. "That's what I hoped it would mean. We've all lost something this year, but it doesn't mean we can't find hope in what's ahead."

Maggie looked at him, the truth of his words sinking into her heart. He was right. They had both lost—Bill, the factory, the future they had once envisioned—but there was still something ahead. It wasn't clear, and it wasn't perfect, but it was there. And maybe that was enough.

"Sam," Maggie said, her voice barely above a whisper, "I don't know what's next. I don't know how things are going to go from here. But I want to try. I want to... move forward."

Sam smiled, a soft, understanding smile. "You don't have to figure it all out tonight, Maggie. One step at a time."

She nodded, grateful for his steady presence, for the quiet way he reminded her that it was okay not to have all the answers. That it was okay to take things one day at a time.

"I think I can do that," she said, her voice firmer now. "One step at a time."

Sam stood then, offering her his hand. "Come on. Let's go back inside. It's freezing out here."

Maggie laughed softly and took his hand, the warmth of his touch spreading through her as he pulled her to her feet. They stood there for a moment, their hands still clasped, the stars bright above them, the snow soft beneath their feet.

As they walked back toward the church, the sounds of laughter and music drifting out into the night, Maggie felt something shift inside her. It wasn't a grand epiphany, but a quiet sense of peace. A sense that she could face whatever came next, that she could carry her grief and her hope together, that she didn't have to choose one over the other.

The Silent Season: A 1950s Christmas Tale of Love, Loss, and Hope

And as they stepped back into the warmth of the church, surrounded by the people who had become their community, Maggie realized that this was her Christmas gift—the grace to let go of the past without losing it, and the strength to move forward without fear.

The night was quiet, but within that quiet was a new kind of light—a light she hadn't thought she would ever find again.

And in that light, Maggie knew she would be okay. One step at a time.

Chapter 9
The Silent Season

Christmas morning came quietly, the world outside Maggie's window blanketed in fresh snow that shimmered under the pale light of dawn. She lay in bed for a moment, listening to the soft hum of the house—the familiar creaks of the floorboards, the faint whistle of the wind against the windows, the peaceful breathing of her children still fast asleep in their room. It was a stillness she hadn't experienced in years, a kind of peace she hadn't believed possible since Bill's death.

When Maggie finally rose, she moved carefully through the house, not wanting to wake Tommy and Susie just yet. The small tree they had decorated together sat in the corner of the living room, its few ornaments glinting softly in the early light. There were only a handful of gifts beneath the tree, each one wrapped in simple paper she had managed to scrape together, but it didn't feel lacking. There was no abundance, no grand show of festivity—but that didn't matter.

Christmas had arrived in its quiet way, and this year, it felt different. It felt... enough.

Maggie made her way to the kitchen, lighting the stove and

The Silent Season: A 1950s Christmas Tale of Love, Loss, and Hope

starting the coffee. She stood by the window as it brewed, watching the snow fall softly outside, painting the world in white. The stillness of the town mirrored something inside her—a sense of calm, of settling into this new version of her life. There was grief, yes, but it wasn't all-consuming anymore. It lived alongside something else—something that felt like hope.

It wasn't the kind of hope she had once known. It wasn't full of expectation or plans for the future. It was quieter, gentler. The kind of hope that came with knowing she had made it through the darkest days and was still standing, still moving forward.

As the coffee brewed, she allowed her thoughts to drift back to the night before. The Christmas pageant had been a success—modest, humble, but beautiful in its own way. Watching Tommy and Susie on stage, hearing the laughter and applause from the townspeople who had gathered despite the hardships of the year, had filled her with a warmth she hadn't expected. It was more than just the spirit of Christmas—it was the realization that they had all made it through this year together, in small but significant ways.

And then there was Sam. Maggie's mind lingered on the conversation they had shared outside the church after the pageant, sitting together in the cold, watching the stars. His quiet strength had been a balm to her in ways she hadn't realized she needed. He understood her grief, not just because he had known Bill, but because he carried his own kind of loss. They hadn't needed to speak much—just being there, in that shared space of understanding, had been enough.

Maggie poured herself a cup of coffee and took it to the living room, settling into the old armchair by the tree. The house was still, the only sound the ticking of the clock on the wall. She took a deep breath, feeling the weight of the year finally beginning to lift from her shoulders. For the first time in months, maybe even years, she felt like she could exhale.

After a while, the sound of small footsteps in the hallway broke the quiet. Maggie smiled to herself as Susie and Tommy padded into the living room, their faces lighting up when they saw the tree and the few gifts underneath it.

"Merry Christmas, Mommy!" Susie called, her voice bright with excitement.

"Merry Christmas," Maggie replied, setting down her coffee and pulling her children into a warm hug. She held them for a moment, savoring the feeling of their small arms around her, the love that filled the room.

They sat down together by the tree, Susie eagerly reaching for the first present. There weren't many, but the children didn't seem to mind. Their joy came not from the number of gifts but from the fact that they were all there, together, sharing in the simple beauty of the day.

As the children opened their presents, Maggie found herself reflecting on how much had changed since last Christmas. A year ago, she had been lost in her grief, barely able to make it through the holiday season without breaking down. But this year, despite everything—the financial struggles, the loss of the factory, the absence of Bill—there was a quiet sense of renewal.

Tommy's eyes lit up as he unwrapped the small book she had managed to find for him at the secondhand store. Susie squealed with delight at the handmade doll Maggie had spent nights stitching together, her small hands eagerly running over its soft yarn hair.

It wasn't much, but their joy was real. And for the first time in a long time, Maggie didn't feel guilty about not being able to give them more. She had given them what mattered—love, stability, the hope that things would get better, even if it wasn't all at once.

As the children played with their new toys, Maggie found herself thinking about what lay ahead. The town was still struggling, the future uncertain. The factory hadn't reopened, and there were no guarantees that things would improve anytime soon. But there was a resilience here, in this small community, that gave her hope. They had weathered this storm together, and they would continue to do so.

Later that morning, a knock at the door broke the peaceful quiet of the house. Maggie's heart skipped slightly, wondering who could be visiting so early on Christmas Day. When she opened the door, Sam stood there, a soft smile on his face, his hands holding a small basket covered in a red and white checkered cloth.

"Merry Christmas, Maggie," he said, his voice warm against the cold air.

"Merry Christmas, Sam," she replied, stepping aside to let him in.

Sam entered, his presence bringing with it a quiet warmth. He set the basket on the kitchen table, and Maggie's curiosity got the better of her. She lifted the cloth to find a small assortment of food—fresh bread, homemade jam, a small pie.

"I thought you and the kids might like a little something extra for today," Sam explained, his voice casual but his eyes searching hers. "It's not much, but... I wanted to do something."

Maggie's heart swelled at the gesture. "Sam, this is... thank you. You didn't have to do this."

He shrugged, a little sheepish. "I wanted to. Besides, I figured we could all use a little more cheer today."

Maggie smiled, the warmth spreading through her. "You're right. We could."

The children, drawn by the sound of Sam's voice, ran into the kitchen, their faces lighting up when they saw him. "Sam! Did you come to see our presents?" Susie asked eagerly.

"I sure did," Sam replied with a grin, kneeling down to their level. "Show me what you got."

As the children excitedly pulled him into the living room, Maggie watched from the kitchen, her heart full. Sam had become more than just a friend over the past few months—he had become *part of their lives in a way she hadn't expected. And standing there, watching him laugh with her children, Maggie realized that she was no longer afraid of that.*

The rest of the day unfolded in quiet contentment. Sam stayed for a simple Christmas lunch, the children's laughter filling the house as they played with their toys and told him all about the pageant from the night before. The hours passed easily, the weight of grief and hardship lifted, even if only for a little while.

As evening fell, the children grew sleepy, and Maggie tucked them into bed with the same soft lullaby she had sung to them since they were babies. When she returned to the living room, Sam was standing by the window, looking out at the snow-covered streets. His expression was thoughtful, quiet, as if he was lost in his own reflections of the day.

Maggie joined him, standing beside him in the soft glow of the tree lights. For a moment, they just stood there, side by side, watching the peaceful snowfall outside.

"I was thinking," Sam said after a while, his voice low, "this Christmas... it's different, isn't it?"

Maggie nodded, her heart full. "Yes. It's quiet, but... it feels right."

Sam looked at her then, his eyes searching hers. "Maggie, I don't know what the future holds for any of us. But I know that... I want to be part of whatever comes next. With you. With the kids."

Maggie's breath caught, her heart skipping a beat at the quiet, earnest way he spoke. There was no rush, no grand declaration— just a simple truth, offered with the same steady kindness that had carried her through the past few months.

She reached for his hand, her fingers finding his in the quiet. "I'd like that, Sam," she said softly, her voice full of sincerity. "I'd like that very much."

As they stood there together, the snow falling softly outside, Maggie felt something settle inside her. It wasn't the kind of peace

The Silent Season: A 1950s Christmas Tale of Love, Loss, and Hope

that erased all the hardship or grief, but it was a beginning. A new kind of hope, one built on the quiet strength of shared burdens and the promise of a future—whatever that might look like.

And for the first time in a long time, Maggie wasn't afraid of what came next. She was ready.

Ready to face the silent season, and whatever lay beyond it, with grace.

With love.

With hope.

Chapter 10
A New Year of Hope

The clock on the mantle ticked softly, its rhythmic beat filling the quiet of the small living room. The tree in the corner, its modest decorations catching the glow of the fire, stood as a gentle reminder of the Christmas that had passed just a few days before. Outside, the snow continued to fall in a steady, silent dance, blanketing the town in a soft hush. It was New Year's Eve, and for the first time in a long while, Maggie felt something she hadn't allowed herself to feel in over a year: hope.

Tommy and Susie were already in bed, their voices having quieted after an evening of whispered excitement about the new year to come. The fire had dwindled to a soft glow, the last embers crackling quietly, and Maggie sat in her favorite chair, staring into the flames. She should have felt the weight of the year's struggles—the loss of the factory, the endless worry about money, the aching absence of Bill that had hovered over every day. But tonight, all she felt was a calm stillness. As if the year was finally letting go, leaving room for something new.

The wooden heart Sam had given her sat on the small table beside her, its surface smooth and familiar under her fingertips. She

The Silent Season: A 1950s Christmas Tale of Love, Loss, and Hope

picked it up, turning it over in her hands, feeling the warmth of the gesture, the weight of what it symbolized—both the pain and the possibility that lay ahead.

Her thoughts drifted to the days since Christmas. It had been quiet, but good. The children had laughed more, smiled more. The house, once so full of silence, had been filled with their voices, their games, their laughter. And then there was Sam—his steady presence had been a balm, easing the loneliness she had carried for so long. There was something unspoken between them, something that didn't need to be rushed or defined, but it was there, and it gave her a sense of peace.

But as much as things had changed, there were still moments when the loss of Bill weighed on her. Sitting by the fire, in the quiet of the night, Maggie allowed herself to remember him. She remembered his laugh, the way his eyes crinkled at the corners when he smiled, the way his arms felt around her. She let herself feel the grief, but this time it didn't crush her. It was a part of her, but it didn't define her anymore.

Her heart ached with the memory, but it was a tender ache, one softened by time and the new memories she was making with her children. With Sam. She had survived the worst year of her life, and as the clock ticked toward midnight, she felt herself letting go of the fear that had gripped her since Bill's death. She could feel something shifting inside her—a readiness to move forward, not by forgetting Bill, but by honoring him in the way she lived her life. By finding joy where she could. By embracing what lay ahead.

A soft knock at the door pulled her from her thoughts. Maggie's heart quickened, and she knew who it was before she even opened it. She made her way to the door, her pulse steady but strong, and when she pulled it open, there stood Sam, bundled against the cold, his cheeks flushed from the winter air.

"Maggie," he said, his voice warm in the icy night. "I hope it's not too late."

She smiled, shaking her head. "No, not at all. Come in."

Sam stepped inside, brushing the snow from his coat, and the warmth of the fire quickly enveloped him. He stood there for a moment, taking in the quiet of the house, the soft glow of the tree, the way Maggie stood in the doorway, her eyes bright and filled with something he hadn't seen before.

"I was just out for a walk," he said, his voice low and steady. "I've been thinking about... this year. About everything we've been through."

Maggie nodded, her heart racing with a quiet intensity. She had been thinking about it too, about how much had changed, how much she had changed.

"I didn't want the year to end without seeing you," Sam continued, his eyes softening. "Without telling you how much you've meant to me. These last few months... they've been hard for all of us, but being with you and the kids—it's given me hope again."

Maggie's breath caught in her throat, her heart swelling with emotion. She had known, on some level, that Sam had become an important part of her life, but hearing him say it out loud, with such quiet sincerity, made the weight of the moment settle deep in her chest.

"I feel the same way, Sam," she said, her voice trembling slightly. "I didn't think I'd ever feel... anything again. After Bill... after everything, I didn't think there could be room for anything else. But you've been here. Steady. You've been here for me and for the kids. And I can't tell you how much that's meant."

Sam took a step closer, his eyes never leaving hers. "You don't have to," he said softly. "I've been right where I need to be."

Maggie felt the warmth of his words settle deep within her, filling the spaces that had been empty for so long. She reached out, her hand finding his, and the connection between them—this quiet, steady bond they had built—felt like the beginning of something solid and real.

The Silent Season: A 1950s Christmas Tale of Love, Loss, and Hope

The clock chimed softly from the mantle, and Maggie glanced over, realizing that midnight was only moments away. The fire crackled softly in the hearth, and the world outside seemed to pause, as if waiting for the new year to make its quiet entrance.

Sam squeezed her hand gently, and she turned back to him, her heart full. "It's almost midnight," she whispered, her voice barely audible in the stillness.

Sam smiled, his eyes full of warmth. "A new year," he said. "A new beginning."

Maggie nodded, her heart swelling with emotion. She had survived the silent season, the long, dark winter of grief and loss, and now, standing here with Sam, she felt ready to face whatever came next. It wouldn't be easy. There would be hard days, moments of sadness, times when she missed Bill with an intensity that took her breath away. But there would also be joy. There would be love. There would be a future.

And for the first time in a long time, Maggie was ready to embrace it.

As the clock struck midnight, Sam leaned in slowly, his breath warm against her cheek. Their kiss was soft, tentative, a promise of something more. It wasn't rushed or full of urgency—it was quiet, just like everything else between them. But it was real. And it was full of hope.

When they pulled away, Maggie's eyes were filled with tears, but they weren't tears of sadness. They were tears of gratitude. For this moment, for this man who had come into her life when she hadn't known she needed him. For the children upstairs, for the town that had come together, for the quiet resilience that had carried them through the hardest year of their lives.

"Maggie," Sam said, his voice a soft whisper in the quiet room. "I don't know what this next year will bring. But I know I want to face it with you. With all of you."

Maggie smiled through her tears, her heart so full she thought it might burst. "I want that too, Sam. I'm ready."

They stood there for a moment, the weight of the new year settling around them, the fire crackling softly, the world outside wrapped in silence.

Maggie felt something shift inside her, a quiet certainty that had been growing for months now. She had survived the storm. She had carried the weight of her grief, her loss, her uncertainty—and now, she was ready to move forward. Not by forgetting, but by remembering, by honoring what had been and embracing what could be.

As they stood together, their hands still clasped, Maggie knew with a quiet, unwavering certainty that the silent season had come to an end. And in its place, there was hope. There was love. There was a future, waiting to unfold one day at a time.

And she was ready. Ready to face it, ready to embrace it, ready to live it.

With Sam. With her children. With all the quiet strength she had found in herself.

The new year had arrived, and with it, the promise of something beautiful.

One step at a time.

Together.

Afterword: The Quiet Before the Storm

As I write this afterword, I'm thinking back to where Maggie's story began—beneath the weight of grief, the cold grip of loss, and the silence of a small town that had forgotten how to breathe. When we first met her, she was a woman on the edge of despair, facing a Christmas season that seemed impossible to survive. And yet, through the course of this quiet journey, Maggie found not only the strength to carry on but also the courage to rebuild. She discovered love in unexpected places, hope in the most ordinary moments, and a future that, while uncertain, was full of promise.

But as much as Maggie's story feels like a journey completed, there are whispers of something more just over the horizon.

The town, though resilient, remains fragile. The factory, still closed, looms over them all like a dark cloud, and while Maggie has found solace in her children and her growing bond with Sam, there are still challenges she cannot foresee. A year can change so much, but what happens when old wounds open again, when new obstacles arise? What happens when the quiet peace she has worked so hard to build is suddenly threatened?

Afterword: The Quiet Before the Storm

As spring gives way to summer and the seasons begin their steady march toward next winter, I find myself wondering, just as you might be: what lies ahead for Maggie and her small town? Will the promise of new beginnings hold, or will the weight of the past come calling again?

And as for Sam, the man who quietly walked into Maggie's life when she needed him most—what secrets does he carry beneath that calm exterior? What will happen if those unspoken parts of him begin to surface, revealing layers Maggie hasn't yet seen? He's been her rock, her anchor, but what if there's more to his story than either of them realize?

The town, too, has its share of unspoken stories—neighbors who have watched in silence, families who struggle behind closed doors, and perhaps even the factory itself, waiting for the day when its gates might reopen... or not. Can the community come together once more in the face of whatever challenges lie ahead, or will the bonds they've forged prove fragile when tested by the unknown?

I can't say for certain what will happen next Christmas. But I know this: Maggie's journey is far from over.

As the snow begins to fall once again in the months to come, and as Christmas approaches next year, there will be new challenges to face, new joys to discover, and perhaps even more heartbreak along the way. But Maggie is no longer the woman she was. She's stronger now, wiser, and ready to face whatever comes next.

For now, we'll leave Maggie, Sam, and the children in the warmth of a spring morning, their hearts full of hope, their hands ready to plant the seeds of a new season. But when the next Christmas rolls around—when the silent season comes again—we'll return to see what has blossomed, and what new trials will emerge.

So, until next year, let's hold on to the quiet joy of this moment. But don't be fooled by the stillness. Change is coming. And with it, a new chapter in Maggie's life—one that might surprise us all.

Stay warm, and until we meet again next Christmas...

www.ingramcontent.com/pod-product-compliance
Lightning Source LLC
LaVergne TN
LVHW050026080526
838202LV00069B/6933